Open Your Heart

God Bless you,

A Devotional Journal

John 3:17

Rance White

Rance R. White

Poetry in Pictures
Belgrade, Minnesota

Copyright © 2006
Rance White

All rights reserved. No part of this book may be reproduced in any form, except for the inclusion of brief quotations in a review, without permission in writing from the author or publisher.

All scripture references are from the KJV.

ISBN 978-0-9790612-0-2

First printing -- 1,000 copies -- November 2006

Additional copies of this book are available by mail.
Send $12.95 each, plus $3.25 shipping,
(plus 6.5% tax in Minnesota) to:
Poetry in Pictures
P.O. Box 726
Belgrade, Minnesota 56312
Visit us on the web @ www.poetryinpictures.com

Printed in the U.S.A. by
Morris Publishing
3212 East Highway 30
Kearney, Nebraska 68847
1-800-650-7888

Dedication

This book is dedicated to my wife, and life partner, Dorreen, without whom this would have never happened. Through patience and commitment we have grown together in the Lord. We pray that you would be blessed, encouraged, and strengthened in your faith.

ACKNOWLEDGMENTS

I wish to thank a few people for their invaluable assistance.

The effort put into the original manuscript by Sally Skramstad Petersen was, and is, priceless. Her editorial gift and wholehearted enthusiasm proved to be an inspirational combination.

The illustrations were provided by two of my children. Thank you, Karn White and Chris White. I'm so glad we could share this.

Special thanks to my wonderful wife, who truly is, my inspiration. Her encouragement has greatly contributed to the development of this book. Her aid in proofreading and editing the final draft of this manuscript was integral to the professional look and feel of the finished book.

I would also like to thank Whitney White and William White for their encouragement and for putting up with me during these hectic days.

Without these people, and others too numerous to mention, this book would not be what it is.

Contents

Acknowledgments..iv
Preface... viii

1. I Love You

Sunday's Coming..2

2. He is Risen

Just Think 6

3. Suffer the Little Children

Rest in His Love..10
You are Loved..12
Promise of Joy...14

4. Our Heart Knows

Truth Hurts Hearts..18

5. Comfort and Hope

Comfort..22
Love Wins..24
Remember; Rejoice...............................26
Legacy of Life.......................................28
Always in My Heart..............................30

6. She Pondered in Her Heart

Loss of a Child......................................34
Wings..36
His Reply...38
Enwrapped in Love...............................40

7. True Friend

True Friend...44
Missing You..46

8. We Stand Upon the Threshold

Walk in Wisdom....................................50
Not Alone..52
Free at Last..54
True Trust...56

9. To Love and Adore

Precious in His Sight............................60
I'll Love You Forever............................ 62
Daddy's Little Girl.................................64

Never Stop Loving You..66
Celebrate..68
Shining Star..70
Greatest...72
Dear Son..74
Forever and Ever..76
Quiet Ways..78
Treasure the Times..80
Treasured Souls..82
When God Called...84
Open Your Heart..86
Because You are You...88
You Were Chosen...90

10. Flesh of My Flesh

Thank-You...94
My Treasure..96
Love Letter..98
Meant to Last...100
A Time of Love...102
Two to One...104
Pot of Gold..106
Question for You..108

11. Free at Last

New Song...112
Amazing Grace...114
Redemption...116
God's Grace..118
Patiently Waiting...120
A New Song..122
Father Knows Best..124

Preface

My pride and stubbornness kept God at arms length. We exchanged pleasantries in passing – and I called this my relationship with God. It wasn't until recently God finally broke through my rough exterior and all of the barriers I had erected.

Through patience and perseverance, God chipped away at the wall between Him and me. What you read on these pages is really the result of that process; an illustration of how He never gives up and can do the impossible.

I've been a Christian for 25 years, and during that time I've been a student of the Bible and read a lot of books. Because of this, I have acquired a lot of knowledge about God. But, the relationship I longed for didn't seem to be progressing. I didn't feel any closer to God. *Walk by faith* was my credo. God said it. I believe it. And that settles it.

I can point to a number of things God has done in the last seven years to bring me to this point. Each event was designed to wear away at my wall until there was finally a breach, and He could reach the inner man of my heart.

My writing started about two years ago. I thank God for the trials He brought into my life to break my heart so He could heal it. I don't own the words on these pages. I just write what God gives me. If these words speak to you, it's because they are empowered by the Spirit of God.

Since I didn't set out to write a book, I believe these are writings God wanted to share. So, don't settle for a superficial relationship with God. Open your heart, and let Him break it, to heal it.

Peace and Love,

Rance

I Love You

Sunday Is Coming

The day began like any other day;
How could we know it would end this way?
I'll see if I can get this right:
It all just happened so fast that night.
The air was festive, full of jubilation
Jerusalem was the place to be, on this day of celebration.
The town was buzzing, the people talked;
Everyone stood and stared as the Master walked.
My heart swelled up -- so full of pride;
Jesus was here, and I at His side.
As we sat down to eat in the upper room,
The Masters' words spoke clearly of doom.
I was stunned and tried making sense of it all;
Surely *my* Master, could never fall.
What's this He's saying about bread and wine?
Body and blood ... broken, betrayal time?
The night air was cool as we went out and walked;
We wrestled our thoughts and nobody talked.
At the garden we all settled in for some rest,
And I prayed that this burden would lift from my chest.
Suddenly, I awoke with a start.
Something was wrong – I knew in my heart.
The soldiers took Jesus away... and I fled;
What was it, at supper, that Jesus had said?
I watched from a distance afraid to go near.
My former bravado revealed only fear.
I watched as Jesus was beaten and mocked;
I stood in amazement, totally shocked.
And, when others said, "Surely you stood at His side."
My Master and Teacher, I three times denied.
I stood as He hung alone on that cross,
And I knew all my hopes and my dreams were now lost.
His body was taken, and laid in the tomb;
As the stone was sealed, so was my gloom.
How can this be? The Messiah has died.
How can it be? He was crucified.

THAT WAS FRIDAY...
BUT SUNDAY IS COMING!

Mark 14:50   And they all forsook him, and fled.

He is Risen

Just Think ...

Three years of my life, I lived with that Man;
He had said, almost daily, that God had a plan.
I watched all the marvelous things that He did;
The joy and the wonder made me feel like a kid.
Would the Messiah do anything this Man hadn't done?
I just knew in my heart that He was the One.
Why, oh why, did He hang on that tree?
Tell me, please tell me: Lord, how can this be?
I knew it would be just a matter of time
Till the soldiers came looking, for me and what's mine.
My heart leapt into my throat in an instant;
As the silence was shattered by pounding, insistent.
If it weren't for the voices that I clearly knew,
My heart would have stopped, and my days been through.
You tell me, that Jesus has caused death to fail?
It's much too early for such outrageous tales!
You gals stay here, while I check this out;
You clearly don't know what you're talking about.
When I got to the tomb, and stepped inside,
The absence of Jesus could not be denied.
The tomb was open; but, with no body inside ...
But it couldn't mean, that He was alive!
I found no relief from my troublesome thoughts;
Just more and more questions for the answers I sought.
The house filled up quickly as more and more came;
More and more people, with similar claims.
Suddenly the room was filled with light;
I stood there, speechless, amazed by the sight.
I felt my knees buckle, and I went down;
He reached out and touched me, as I knelt on the ground.
Peace and love came and flooded my soul;
They rushed out in praises, I just couldn't control.
It seemed as though there were just He and I;
He spoke only of love, as I trembled and cried.
If God can forgive me and make my life new,
...just think... what He could do for you.

Mark 16:6 ... ye seek Jesus of Nazareth, which was crucified: he is risen; he is not here ...

Suffer the Little Children

Rest in His Love

If I could tell you just one thing,
To try to ease your suffering,

I'd try my best to help you see
How Jesus longs to set you free.

He knows your pain; He knows your fear;
Holds out His hands and says, "Draw near".

Take hold of His hands and look in His eyes.
The love you see there just can't be denied!

Fall into His arms, and snuggle up close;
Take joy in the touch of Him who loves you most.

Just rest in His love, and open your heart.
Give yourself time for the healing to start.

Let go of the lies you've believed for so long;
Let His love infuse you -- let Him make you strong!

You're worth much more than diamonds or gold;
Believe in your heart, and He'll make you whole.

John 14:27   Peace I leave with you, my peace I give unto you: ... Let not your heart be troubled, neither let it be afraid.

You Are Loved

God longs to give you joy and peace;
To touch your heart and bring release.

He knows your pain; He knows your grief;
The hurt in your heart that cuts so deep.

He stands beside you with arms open wide...
Says, "Rest in my arms, and together we'll cry."

Your heart's been broken and has been trampled so long,
It may take a while, but I'll make it strong.

The pain and the guilt and shame that you feel;
Are merely illusions that appear to be real.

The enemy comes to steal, kill, and destroy;
He puts pain in your heart and robs you of joy.

You've lived long enough in his shadow of lies;
Let Jesus love you and He'll heal your mind.

You are more precious than silver or gold,
And glory and honor, and riches untold.

So look unto Jesus, and open your heart;
Give way to His love, let the healing start.

John 12:46   I am come a light into the world, that whosoever believeth on me should not abide in darkness.

Promise of Joy

How can I tell you how much Jesus cares,
To know how He longs to break through your despair?

Your heart has been tied up and locked up so long;
You don't even know that your thoughts aren't your own.

The enemy comes to steal, kill, and destroy;
He's kidnapped your heart and made it his toy.

You want to believe that you're in control,
But, truth be told, you're far, far from whole.

That world in your mind, you believe to be real
Has taken and shaped the things that you feel.

Examine your feelings and please, ask yourself;
Are your feelings intent on destroying yourself?

You are of great value; a pearl of great price;
Don't let Satan destroy you by telling you lies.

This life holds the promise of joy and of love,
Happiness, faith, and hope from above.

So, how can I tell you how much Jesus cares;
To know how He longs to break through your despair?

Psalm 27:1   The Lord is my light and my salvation; whom shall I fear? The Lord is the strength of my life; of whom shall I be afraid?

Our Heart Knows

Truth Hurts Hearts

How many children have been sacrificed
on the altar of convenience and greed?

How many times has a heart been stopped
by someone who claimed to be free?

We say it's our right, we have the choice,
to silence that little ones' voice.

Don't confuse us with facts about hearts, lungs, and feet,
or claims that a fetus feels pain.

Don't try to guilt us into changing our minds
with a walk down *your* memory lane...

As long as we can remain detached and
call it a routine procedure,

We can bury our feelings and
deny the guilt and shame.

But all we've done is lie to ourselves,
with our voices that scream and shout:

For deep in our hearts, the truth still remains;
and the emptiness can't be denied.

We had our procedure, we tell ourselves,
but our hearts know: This baby has died.

Psalm 139:16 ... and in thy book all my members were written... when as yet there was none of them.

Comfort and Hope

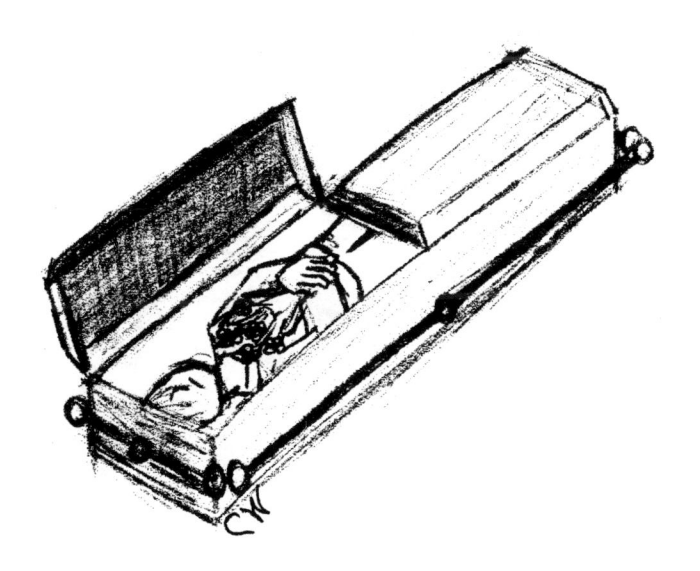

Comfort

I go through the motions, day by day;
Friends stumble and falter; not knowing what to say.

They don't know what I feel, or what goes on in my head,
They just know you were here, and that now you are dead.

There's so much pain inside, I just want to hide.
My heart screams out "Why?
 Why was it *you* that had to die?"
"Why are *you* gone and I'm left here to cry?"

My head is spinning and my knees are weak.
I'm so exhausted, I can't even think.

My soul is sinking into despair;
I keep sinking deeper, and gasping for air.

At night when the darkness begins to close in,
And the world becomes quiet and still...

Sorrow and loneliness come crashing in,
And threaten to engulf me until:

My Savior reminds me that He is still here!
He'll never leave me; He'll always be near.

So I crawl into His outstretched arms;
Lay my head in his lap and cry.

John 11:25 ... I am the resurrection and the life: He that believeth in me, though he were dead, yet shall he live:

Love Wins

I felt the need to be close, my friend;
So today, I read your letters again.

I curled up in my favorite overstuffed chair;
And felt just like a hibernating bear.

I dusted off old memories that had faded with time,
And my heart rejoiced when they came alive.

I could see your face -- I could hold your hand...
For now we were together again.

Your love washed over me, from deep down inside;
It felt so good, I laughed 'til I cried.

We stepped out together and walked back in time;
We shared precious moments, and we laughed and we cried.

I joyed in your presence and my heart was revived;
I know you'll be waiting when I reach the other side.

Friends may come and friends may go.
But love will never die.
Love is the reason,
I don't have to say good-bye.

I John 2:25 And this is the promise that he hath promised us, even eternal life.

Remember; Rejoice!

Our world is diminished through the loss of light;
The light that was _____, who burned so bright.
Picture ____ there with ____ radiant smile;
      him/her   his/her
As you dwelt in the warmth of ___ love for a while.
                                   his/her
This precious gift from God above;
Burned bright with the fullness of His love.

We are the lucky ones; you and me;
For we were blessed to know _____.

Our lives have been touched; our hearts have been changed;
Because of ____ presence in this world of pain.
       his/her
With arms open wide, and ____ heart open too;
                          his/her
_____ was never too busy to help pull you through.
He/She

Living life to the fullest, somehow _____ knew;
                               he/she
To make life complete, there had to be you.

With a life that was lived in service to others,
_____ quickly acquired many "sisters and brothers".
He/She

Oh, the treasures stored up in _____ heart;
                          his/her
In which you and I each played a part.

In the presence of Jesus, _____ opens _____ heart;
                         he/she   his/her
As tears fill ____ eyes, the praises start.
      his/her
Now, the words of the Master to one He adores:
"Look around you, my child; great is your reward."

I Corinthians 13:13   And now abideth faith, hope, charity, these three; but the greatest of these is charity.

Legacy of Life

What is the true measure of a man?
What makes him great? What makes him grand?

Is honor attained through advancement in years?
Or is wisdom bestowed on those with gray beards?

Does mere passage of time mean a life well-lived?
Or is it measured more aptly in how much we give?

No man is an island, left unto himself;
A life spent on others yields untold wealth.

The legacy of life begins with one...
And is passed on to others, through daughters and sons...

And fathers and mothers, sisters and brothers;
People at work; friends -- even others.

All together share a common bond;
Their lives were touched, somehow, by this one.

Though the body has gone to dust whence it came;
Love lives forever, in our hearts, day to day.

In the words of the Master to one He adores:
"Look around you, my child, great is your reward."

Revelation 22:12   And, behold, I come quickly; and my reward is with me, to give to every man according as his work shall be.

Always in my Heart

Lord, what's happened to my heart?
Why do I feel such pain?

I know my heart is broken,
And can never be the same.

The time we had together
Was but a whisper in the dark.

How can one so small and frail
Dig so deep into my heart?

From the very moment I knew
That life within me grew,

I marveled at your gift of love,
As life became brand-new …

No longer just my selfish thoughts,
Of, me, myself, and I.

My world was then expanding,
To include a baby's sigh.

But my world was cruelly shattered
When my baby did not sigh.

Not a moan or a whisper;
A whimper or a cry.

Before I even said hello,
I was forced to say good-bye.

Revelation 21:4   And God shall wipe away all tears from their eyes; and there shall be no more death, neither sorrow, nor crying, neither shall there be any more pain: ...

And She Pondered in Her Heart

Loss of a Child

The angels are singing as heaven rejoices,
And with heaven's host, we lift up our voices.

_____ life made God's presence known;
But now God has called His servant home.

A life can't be measured in length of days;
God uses each life in His own special way.

Can we grieve? Can we be sad?
I dare to ask – can we even be mad?

God understands our pain and our grief;
Remember, His Son died like a thief.

God can handle your questions and doubt,
For He understands what life is about.

Don't bury our feelings-- that's how we feel;
Love without pain can never be real.

But, while we are hurting, remember to sing!
Remember the love and joy _____ brings!

God has given us an amazing gift:
This precious soul to share life with.

I Corinthians 15:55   O death, where is thy sting? O grave, where is thy victory?

Wings

Today we place into Gods' arms;
Our precious bundle, full of charm.

We lift you up to God in prayer;
At His altar, as we place you there.

God has placed you in our care
And given us your life to share.

We feel so blessed and are so proud
To share the joy in you we've found.

The moment we first saw your face,
We knew the fullness of God's grace...

A grace so deep and without measure,
That has given us so great a treasure.

So, walk with us along life's road,
And give to us your hand to hold.

We'll walk together, three in one;
Just like the Father, Spirit, Son.

Let our love lift you to the sky;
'Till your own wings,
 Are strong enough to fly.

Luke 2:22 ... they brought him to Jerusalem, to present him to the Lord.

His Reply

One day I prayed within my heart;
I asked my Father where to start...

"Where to start? My child, you see,
You need to put your faith in me."

"You shared your love; you opened your heart;
You gave your child the perfect start."

"Amazing love, how can it be?
You introduced your child to me."

"The words you planted long ago;
In fertile ground, indeed still grow."

"My words went forth to do their task;
What I command will come to pass."

"Two hearts once beating on their own;
Have joined as one to make a home."

"Into this home, I placed a wee one;
To point the way, so they may come."

"Now you and I can celebrate;
Let's let them know that this is great!"

"My heart is filled with love, you see;
When I see this family."

Psalm 126:6   He that goeth forth and weepeth, bearing precious seed, shall countless come again with rejoicing, bringing his sheaves with him.

Enwrapped in Love

I sense again that familiar rush
That bids me pause, be still, and hush.

There's no warning, no tell - tale sign;
Just the urgency of this point in time.

My body is telling me, once again,
That what I have will never mend.

Our bodies are priceless works of art;
But, how does one live with defective parts?

I said my prayers, I made my peace;
Thinking my soul would be released.

I cry out to God, and He draws near;
Says "Listen, my child, and you shall hear…"

"The song that you were made to sing
Can only be sung in suffering."

"Your life is more than flesh and blood --
your life is spirit enwrapped in love."

"Whenever you struggle, there's help from above,
Remember, my child, that God is love."

II Corinthians 12:9 ... my grace is sufficient for thee: for my strength is made perfect in weakness.

True Friend

True Friend

Unconditional love, devoted friendship;
Who comes running when you open your door?

Utter devotion, total acceptance;
Who's this dancing across the floor?

Wide - eyed with excitement, body shaking,
Just aching to greet you and to say, hello...

Wants to be near you, heart is racing;
So happy to see you, don't you know?

Doesn't blame you for not being there,
Get angry, or pout: never shuts you out.

_____ wants you to know _____ has love to share;
He/she   he/she
Being with you is what _____ life is about.
                     his/her
Not afraid to love or to be loved in return;
Breaks down your defenses: you smile without concern.

Open your heart as you watch _____ squirm;
                            him/her
Relax and forget about life for a term.

At times it seems that we tend to forget --
Life is much sweeter when you have a pet.

Proverbs 17:17   A friend loveth at all times, and a brother is born for adversity.

Missing You

The price of love sometimes runs steep,
And hurts you to the core.

This pain within my heart's so great
I just can take no more.

You were my true companion --
You were my one best friend.

To live this life without you now...
I wish mine, too, would end.

If, through love, you enter heaven,
I know that you are there,

For, greater love, I've never known
Than that which we have shared.

I miss the warmth within your eyes,
Your nose, your tail, your hair.

I even miss the little things;
The way you were just there.

I miss you, my dear friend.

Matthew 5:4   Blessed are they that mourn: for they shall be comforted.

We Stand Upon the Threshold

Walk in Wisdom

In the wisdom of prophets and sages I've read,
Life's greatest concern is which path to tread.

You don't need to walk paths of sorrow and dread;
You can find peace and contentment instead.

There's a book that guides you through its text
With wisdom, knowledge, and enlightenment.

To illumine our minds, lest we forget:
There's a light within and a light ahead.

When two become one, your fears can be shed;
You'll move on in confidence, as you are led.

Just, step out in faith, in the blood that was shed
By Jesus, the Christ, who rose from the dead.

Like a lamb to the slaughter, our Savior was led,
So that you may have life abundant instead.

Psalm 119:11   Thy word have I hid in mine heart …

Not Alone

We stand upon the threshold and the promise of tomorrow,
And we view the dotted landscapes: love and pain; joy and sorrow.

The years of preparation which have brought us to this place,
Serve only as our stepping stones, to help us run the race.

The richness and the blessing of families that care --
Mothers, fathers, sisters, brothers; the heritage we share.

And as to friends, just let me ask, "Who among us walks alone"?
If not for kindred spirits, this world could not be home.

Have you a special someone, who makes you feel alive...
When you bask in the warmth of their sweet love, as they beam with pride?

We do not live our lives unto ourselves alone;
We're surrounded by a vast array of witnesses untold.

Let us take a moment to reflect on who we are,
For in our inner recesses, there lies a shining star.

So let us step out in courage, confidence and trust;
For as we walk with love's support, you know succeed we must.

The very selfsame forces that have brought us to this day.
Are here to help and guide us as we journey on our way.

Hebrews 12:1 Wherefore seeing we also are compassed about with so great a cloud of witnesses ...

Free at Last

When I was young and full of myself,
I just couldn't appreciate anyone else.

I could not listen to sound advice
My heart was hard and cold as ice.

But now that youthful years have passed,
I find my heart is free at last.

Free to invest in the lives of others:
Sisters and wives, husbands and brothers.

Free to love, and love in return;
To give of my heart, for love is *not* earned.

The voices of those who have gone on before
Are calling me now as never before.

They say in this life, there's more than just me;
I'm only a part of a vast company.

There's nothing I do just unto myself;
All that I do affects someone else.

Each day brings a choice; so, what shall I do?
Revert to myself, or reach out to You?

I'll make it a point to reach out to You;
For life's greatest blessings occur when I do.

Proverbs 11:14   Where no counsel is, the people fall: but in the multitude of counselors there is safety.

True Trust

I step out in faith with fear and trembling,
And look to you, Lord, to supply my needs.

If I am to believe, without a doubt,
Then I must make a move, I must step out.

God, I believe you have called me especially to this;
So, help me to know that it's not just *my* wish.

If only, my Lord, we could speak face to face;
If you'd only come down and meet me some place...

My ears wish to hear; my eyes wish to see;
My hands wish to touch; like Thomas, I'd be.

The world of the Spirit, You say, is as real
As anything here, in this world, that I feel.

The voice of the Lord is heard with my heart;
Please, speak to my heart-- that fear may depart.

The promises of God are sure and true;
He will be with me, whatever I do.

What shall I fear, with God at my side?
I'm not left alone: I follow my Guide.

John 14:26   But the comforter, which is the holy ghost... he shall teach you all things, and bring all things to your remembrance ...

To Love and Adore

Precious in His Sight

For a few short years we're given charge,
We're told to raise the kids as ours.

God has chosen us, elect,
To love and honor, and to protect.

The little ones placed in our care
He's given us the joy to share.

We know not what awaits ahead,
But pray, through Him, our hearts be led.

There will be pain, there will be grief,
There will be joy beyond belief.

Each gift of life, a new creation;
A time for joy, and for adoration.

These lives we touch are not ours to own;
There's more to life than just flesh and bone.

A life can't be measured in length of days;
God uses each life in His own special way.

We watch in love and admiration,
As they fulfill God's aspirations.

God has given us an amazing gift:
These precious souls to share life with.

Psalm 128:3   Thy wife shall be as a fruitful vine by the sides of thine house: thy children like olive plants round about thy table.

I'll Love You Forever

Who is this kid with the mischievous grin,
Who's infectious laughter can draw you right in?

Whose affable charm will steal your heart,
As mine was stolen -- right from the start.

From the moment that you arrived on this earth,
In that wonderful mystery we know as birth...

The years have brought changes as you've grown and matured;
Things happen so quickly, they seem like a blur.

So I tuck precious moments inside my heart,
To help me remember, at least, little parts.

I want to reach out and turn back the clock,
But I'd never be able to decide where to stop.

God has asked me to guide you for a brief point in time;
And be ready to let go when He gives you flight.

I'll cherish the moments that we have together,
Tuck them into my heart and guard them as treasure.

You've made my life richer and fuller by far;
I'll love you forever, just as you are.

Luke 2:19   But Mary kept all these things, and pondered them in her heart.

Daddy's Little Girl

The day of your birth was a special day
Because that's when you entered my heart to stay.

From the very first moment I looked on your face
I sensed in my heart God's amazing grace.

Children are a gift from the Lord;
To have and to hold, to love and adore.

Mere words can't describe the way that I feel...
This love is so strong, it has to be real.

Put these words that I speak deep in your heart,
And know that – forever -- we never will part.

I'll always be here to love and protect you,
And as you grow older, I'll love and respect you.

You began your life crawling, but one day, you'll take flight.
I'll try to release you, and not hold on too tight.

And when you leave to start out on your own,
Just remember your dad, who loves you, at home.

No matter how much you grow and mature,
You'll always just be my little girl.

Psalm 115: 13,14   He will bless them that fear the Lord, both small and great. The Lord shall increase you more and more, you and your children.

Never Stop Loving You

I carry you in my heart each day,
To keep you near, even when you're away.

Years ago you were my little girl,
Always there to whirl and twirl.

I held you tenderly in my arms,
While you pierced my heart with your own special charms.

My heart swelled up, so full of pride,
And joy sprang up from deep inside.

I knew I'd love you forever and ever,
And the end of forever -- happens never!

Now you've grown up and maybe you doubt;
You question this love that I'm talking about.

You ask, "Is it real? Could it really be true?
Do you love me as much as you say that you do?"

Just look in my eyes and you'll know that it's true:
I'll never, no never, stop loving you!

John 15:9   As the Father hath loved me, so have I loved you: continue ye in my love.

Celebrate!

Celebrate! Rejoice! Lift up your voice and sing!
We have been so richly blessed. God has done great things!

Two hearts, once beating on their own, God has joined as one;
And through the gift of love divine, brought forth a little one.

Our hearts are filled with joy and wonder
At this wondrous spell we've fallen under.

Children are gifts right from the Lord;
To have and to hold, love and adore.

One man, one woman, and baby make three;
Have come together to form a family.

'Twas a miracle of God that brought forth this one;
And He holds out His hands and bids you to come.

We join in your joy, and we celebrate;
Just want you to know: we think this is great.

Once again God has spoken, and said to our hearts:
"I've loved you forever, right from the start."

Psalm 127:3   Lo, children are a heritage of the Lord: and the fruit of the womb is his reward.

Shining Star

I'm filled with awe and wonder as I look into your eyes,
And instantly, my heart just melts, when I hear your sighs.

The long awaited day has come, and now you're in my arms;
I feel your love and tenderness burn deep into my heart.

My heart swells up so full of pride, because of who you are;
For you are a part of me; you are my shining star.

I've never known a love so pure, so strong, a love so true;
This new exciting path I'm on, I'm on because of you.

Today we start a journey; we step out hand in hand;
And place ourselves in God's dear care; for we know He has a plan.

I pray that you will dream big dreams, have courage, and be strong;
For God himself will walk with us, as we walk along.

You step into the spotlight, and all the world's a stage;
And all the ones who love you, will help you on your way.

So let me love and guide you and lift you to the sky;
And be the wind beneath your wings as you learn to fly.

Joshua 1:9 ... Be strong and of a good courage; be not afraid, neither be thou dismayed: for the Lord thy God is with thee withersoever thou goest.

Greatest

In joy and wonder, you entered my life,
Melting my heart, as you opened your eyes.

I felt the love within me grow, as I surrendered
to your charms;
I knew my life was forever changed, when I held
you in my arms.

I've never known a love so pure, a love so great, so
grand;
I felt this love spread through my heart, when I first
held your hand.

The fears, the doubts, the wonderings, I harbored for a
while;
Were burned away like the morning mist, in the radiance
of your smile.

My life now has new meaning; your love makes me
strong;
You've filled my life with wonder, you've filled my life
with song.

You are my greatest blessing; you are my greatest joy;
You are my greatest treasure, you are my baby boy.

With hearts forever bound as one and Jesus at our side...
We'll walk together, side by side, in love we cannot hide.

Through the miracle of birth, God shows me once again;
He gives the greatest blessings; He is the great I AM.

Psalm 48:1   Great is the Lord, and greatly to be praised in the city of God, in the mountain of his holiness.

Dear Son

I was there when you first opened your eyes,
And greeted this world with your tiny cries.

My heart opened up and you stepped inside...
All it took was one look into your eyes.

The adventure was starting as life had begun,
For this dear one I called my son.

We stepped out together to face what may come,
Just me and my son, my little one.

We've shared life's successes and some of its sorrows,
We've shared life's joys and painful tomorrows.

We've journeyed together along this same path,
And there's never been cause to show any wrath.

The days have gone by and stretched into years,
Amid the laughter, trials, and tears.

You've followed your heart and let it steer
To a future that's so bright and clear.

Now I stand here with you, to watch what you'll do:
For your heart is steady, and honest, and true.

Whatever your heart may lead you to do,
Remember, my son, I'm so proud of you!

Proverbs 22:6   Train up a child in the way he should go: and when he is old, he will not depart from it.

Forever and Ever

Long ago, before you two held hands,
God above had a master plan.

He opened your hearts and brought you together,
Said, "I'll make of these two, one that is better."

You stood at the altar and faced life together;
Promised your love, forever and ever.

The years have been blessed; the years have been tough;
The years have been kind; and the years have been rough.

The love that you shared made your hearts strong;
When you faced life united, together as one.

You clung to each other as you journeyed along,
And stood on conviction, as you followed the Son.

You started with nothing when you made your first home,
And, over the years, your family has grown.

You were there to watch each new life start:
Hold them, love them, hide them deep in your heart.

Value isn't measured in silver or gold;
The true gifts of God are children to hold.

You promised to love forever and ever,
And, because of that love, great is your treasure!

Luke 1:50   And his mercy is on them that fear him from generation to generation.

Quiet Ways

How to say what's in my heart?
I wouldn't know just where to start.

We've been together many years;
Through love and laughter, pain and tears.

For all my life, you've been there;
Showing me how much you care.

As scenes of remembrance run through my mind,
To my amazement, this I find:

Though I have memories grand in scope,
It's the little things that mean the most.

As I open my heart and open my mind,
I uncover treasures lost in time.

The virtues and morals I now possess,
Were planted by you, in tenderness.

It's not so much the things you said,
It's the quiet way in which you led.

Your life is a model that taught me this truth:
It's not what you say, it's what you do.

Matthew 7:20   Wherefore by their fruits ye shall know them.

Treasure The Times

What does it truly mean to say;
Another year has gone away?

Three hundred sixty - five days have passed,
Since the candles burned, so brightly, last.

Is this a time to stop and reflect?
To immerse ourselves in pain and regret?

Do we mourn the passing of our youth?
Or do we know a deeper truth?

Our lives are but a vapor; a mist;
Take joy in the moments, or you could miss:

The blessing of a loving spouse,
In the sanctuary of your house.

Those precious times of wonderment,
From the children that you are lent.

The memories you hold so dear
When friends and family do draw near.

So, set your mind on things above,
For God has filled your life with love.

Psalm 1:3   And he shall be like a tree planted by the rivers of water, that bringeth forth fruit in his season; his leaf also shall not wither; and whatsoever he doeth shall prosper.

Treasured Souls

God opened His heart and sent forth His love,
And it rained down upon us from heaven above.

To each was given love without measure;
In sharing with others, we bring God pleasure.

The treasured souls that God can trust
Live lives of service because they must.

They give of themselves time and again;
Without even thinking -- because they can.

Just think of the joy God finds in you
As you share His love in all that you do.

Many were blessed because you shared;
Many were blessed because you cared.

As you reach out to others in unselfish love,
You store up your treasure in heaven above.

Not much is certain; but this much is true:
My life has been blessed because of you.

Matthew 23:11　　But he that is greatest among you shall be your servant.

When God Called

When God called, you said yes, you stepped out in faith,
Held to each other and started the race.

You lived in the moment and held tight to His hand;
You knew in your heart that God had a plan.

And because you were faithful and answered the call,
He's made you a light and a blessing to all.

How many lives have been touched by your love,
As you shared, through your lives, the God from above?

Through you, God has healed broken hearts;
Strengthened, enlightened, given courage to start.

You've been on the forefront, Ambassadors for Christ;
Beacons of hope, as you hold forth His light.

You've stood strong through sorrows, struggles, and pain,
As you clung to the Savior in His holy name.

I can't speak for others, but this much is true:
My life has been blessed, because there was you.

Revelation 3:21   To him that overcometh will I grant to sit with me on my throne, even as I also overcame, and am set down with my Father in his throne.

Open Your Heart

Every breath is a gift from God,
Our bodies on loan from Him above.

A life of years: sixty, eighty, more?
Or maybe less, who knows for sure?

We can't control how long we live,
But we can control how much we give.

Our lives are more than flesh and bone
Or the line between dates on a stone.

Bring God with you in your everyday life;
With children, husband, friends, and wife.

In life, we make choices day by day,
In the way we treat others: the things that we say.

It's the little things that mean a lot;
Everyday courtesies time forgot.

Did you live life for others, or just you alone?
What will be left when God calls you home?

Open your heart to those around you, in love;
For you have been blessed by God above.

Psalm 90:12   So teach us to number our days, that we may apply our hearts to wisdom.

Because You Are You

Close your eyes and take a deep breath;
Slow down, relax; take time to reflect.

Count your blessings; name them one by one.
Set your mind on what the Lord has done.

God has made you one of a kind,
So, hold forth your light, and let it shine.

Each day you are given is a gift from above;
Another chance to show forth His love.

As you go through your life, day by day;
Keep your heart open, and you'll hear Him say,

"Thank you for being willing to share.
Thank you for showing them that I care."

"I don't love you for the things that you do --
I love you simply because you are you."

Matthew 5:16   Let your light so shine before men, that they may see your good works and glorify your Father which is in heaven.

You Were Chosen

When I look into your eyes,
To me it comes as no surprise...

The love, compassion, strength and peace,
Which, through you, Jesus has released.

God looks for those that He can use,
To heal the broken, hurt, and bruised.

You have opened your heart to God above,
And let Him fill you with His love...

A love that's vast and knows no bounds,
Embracing all who come around.

Open your heart and pour out your love;
For you were chosen by God above.

I Samuel 16:7 ... for the Lord seeth not as man seeth, for man looketh on the outward appearance, but the Lord looketh on the heart.

Flesh of my Flesh

Thank-You

I just want you to know, what you've done for me...
How your love and encouragement set me free.

Free to pursue my dreams without fear
Simply because of your faith and cheer.

Free from a life of questioning doubt,
You've given me something to smile about.

Free to step out with faith in the Lord;
Two hearts, together, in one accord.

We'll step out together, and follow the Son;
Two souls, together, united as one.

With faith in each other, and faith in our God,
Our path will be blessed from heaven above.

We'll pray in the Spirit, and He'll be our guide;
He'll always be with us, right there at our side.

Just two little words, but they say so much;
Just want to say, Thank You -- so very much.

Psalm 89:1   I will sing of the mercies of the Lord forever: with my mouth will I make known thy faithfulness to all generations.

My Treasure

If I could do it all over again,
I'd marry you like I did back then.

We'd walk down the aisle, hand in hand;
You'd be my girl and I'd be your man.

With love so fresh, so young, so new;
No longer alone, just me, just you.

Love reaches out to me and to you;
Takes both of our hearts and makes one of two.

Love is given so freely, without measure;
To you, my wife, my love, my *treasure.*

As in the words of Jesus – Matt 6:21
"Where your treasure is, there will your heart be also."

Matthew 6:21   For where your treasure is, there will your heart be also.

Love Letter

I look back in my mind through time,
And everywhere I look your face I find.

That smile, the laughter behind your eyes;
That "look" that keeps me mesmerized.

The passage of time has creased your brow;
The once golden mane is silver now.

Each step along the way, I see anew;
The warmth and the love I still find in you.

That love that's been mine in true romance --
Since you captured my heart with just a glance.

From the day that you promised and said "I do";
To this moment in time: I am with you.

The joy I find in my heart today
Was born when you came, and grows as you stay!

Happy Anniversary!

Matthew 19:5 ... For this cause shall a man leave father and mother, and shall cleave to his wife: and they twain shall be one flesh?

Meant to Last

How many times have I asked myself,
"Could I have lived with anyone else"?

One thing the years have come to show:
The answer is a resounding, "No"!

You've touched my heart in such a way
That only makes me want to stay.

You can't enter marriage hoping to change someone;
But changes occur when two hearts become one.

The life I lived before we met
Was to prepare me for the day we met.

My heart was open when it met yours,
And the two created a love that endures.

A love so deep, so wonderful, so true;
It wouldn't have happened if it wasn't for you.

We've grown together along the same path,
And we know our love is meant to last.

Genesis 2:18 And the Lord God said, it is not good that the man should be alone; I will make him a help meet for him.

A Time of Love

A time of love for a few short years,
You stepped into my heart to chase away my fears.

Fears of loneliness; fears of doubt;
Fears of shame, confusion; too many to count.

God looked through time and saw your hand in mine...
Said, "I'll make her for him; and him for her."

"The two of them will be stronger together.
To have and to hold forever and ever."

"They will face life's fears united as one;
And we will be with them as they follow the Son."

God has given me a precious gift;
Someone who stands to say, "I'll go with!"

Thank – you for your commitment.

Ecclesiastes 4:12   And if one prevail against him, two shall withstand him; and a threefold cord is not quickly broken.

Two to One

I've asked myself, a time or two,
If I would know love without you.

With another that I knew,
Would I have found a love so true?

Long ago when time began
God took some dust and formed a man.

God knew man shouldn't live alone,
So He created someone to call his own.

Eve was formed from Adam's rib,
So she could walk alongside of him.

There was no questioning, fear, or doubt;
This was one he couldn't live without.

God made two of one, then one of two;
When He brought me to be with you.

I know I've found my only one;
Because you and I were made from one.

There's someone for everyone;
My one is you.

Genesis 2:22 And the rib, which the Lord God had taken from man, made he a woman, and brought her unto the man.

Pot of Gold

One day there was me,
And one day there was you.

Our hearts came together and made one
of the two.
So now we're together, forever and ever:

The one that was me,
And the one that was you.

Now, the future is bright, so don't you worry.
No need to rush, be in a hurry.

Savor the days as they go past.
We know our love was meant to last.

So, walk with me along life's road.
For in our love is our pot of gold.

Genesis 2:24   Therefore shall a man leave his father and his mother, and shall cleave unto his wife: and they shall be one flesh.

Question for You

I ask you sincerely, what can I do
To prove how great my love is for you?

I could climb over mountains, swim across seas,
If that's what you think love should be.

I could sit by your side and hold your hand
And tell you forever that I am your man.

I could buy you flowers, silver, or gold;
And shower you with riches untold.

I could whisk you away to a faraway land;
And walk with you, barefoot, our toes in the sand.

I could tame wild beasts, the lion, the bear;
And rescue you from the pit of despair.

I could battle the dragon and set you free;
To prove how much you mean to me.

I could promise the moon, the earth and stars;
Celestial bodies, Jupiter, Mars.

Or I could get down on one knee, pull out a ring;
And ask you please – "Will you marry me?"

Song of Solomon 4:1 Behold, thou art fair, my love; behold, thou art fair; ...

Free at Last

New Song

The song in my heart is a song of praise;
My heart wants to worship you all of my days.

You delivered me from a deep, dark pit
And gave to me heavenly citizenship.

My heart was wicked and full of sin;
Till I opened the door and let You walk in.

When You walked into my heart that day,
I knew that love was here to stay.

You planted a seed of something divine;
By fusing Your heart together with mine.

Now the joy that I find in my heart today
Fills up so fast, I must give it away.

Rapturous joy, joy overflowing;
Joy flows out without even knowing.

Is it any wonder that I scream and shout?
I just have to let these feelings out!

I never knew life could be so good;
I'm so glad I moved to your neighborhood.

Psalm 40:2   He brought me up also out of a horrible pit, out of the miry clay, and set my feet upon a rock, and established my goings.

Amazing Grace

Let's explore for a moment the concept of grace,
For without it, the world would explode into space.

We take life for granted, as if it's our right;
As if we, ourselves, supplied our own light.

Life as we know it would cease to exist;
If the balance of nature somehow were to shift.

From the very beginning, God had a plan;
His crowning achievement: the creation of man.

God spoke and the planets, the sun, moon, and stars,
Took their place in space, like Jupiter and Mars.

The world was void and formless, when God spoke again;
And one by one, the changes came, as He gave command.

When the world was ready, in the Garden, God placed man;
And all of God's creation rejoiced as Time began.

One day, in the Garden, the man chose to take a stand;
He thought that maybe, he himself, had a better plan.

Now when the deed transpired, God knew what man had done;
So God sent forth a sacrifice; He sent His only Son.

And through that very sacrifice, provided for the fall,
The gift of His amazing grace, our God extends to all.

John 3:17   For God sent not his son into the world to condemn the world; but that the world through him might be saved.

Redemption

The one true God came in the flesh
And died on a cross to buy our righteousness.

This was determined before time began;
And long before the creation of man.

The salvation of man wasn't an afterthought,
Or a quick response because man had gotten caught.

God knew the price He'd have to pay,
And chose to love us, anyway.

Of the many things He could have done,
He chose to save us with His love.

To God, you're more precious than silver or gold;
Diamonds or pearls, riches untold.

When sin entered the world through Adam and Eve
Blood had to be shed to gain reprieve.

In the fullness of time God brought forth the One;
And you were saved by the blood of God's own Son.

"For God so loved the world that He gave His only begotten Son, that whosoever believes in Him, should not perish but have everlasting life."
John 3:16

Galatians 4:4   But when the fullness of time was come, God sent forth his Son, made of a woman, made under the law,

God's Grace

The world and all the vastness of space
Was placed into orbit through God's dear grace.

God opened His mouth and spoke forth the Word
And the forces of nature obeyed what was heard.

The planets aligned, bursting with pride;
As the sun and stars burned bright in the sky.

The earth was blessed to bring forth life,
Wonder and beauty... an incredible sight!

Through all of creation, God had a plan;
And in the midst of this beauty, God placed man.

He placed man in the garden, and then gave command
That all of creation was subject to man.

God looked at the sight and was filled with delight;
For all was serene, peaceful, and bright.

The man and the woman lived life with God;
And the three, in the garden, together did trod.

Then, one day, God stood in the garden, alone;
He called out to Adam and Eve to come home.

"I know you have sinned, and broken the bond;
But, I haven't changed, my love is still strong."

"You don't have to run and hide from My face;
Your sins are forgiven and covered by grace!"

Genesis 3:9   And the Lord God called unto Adam, And said unto him, Where art thou?

Patiently Waiting

If you want to see the love of God,
Open your heart to open your eyes.

The veil has been lifted, if you just believe;
Without faith it is impossible to see.

Your heart is held hostage, a victim of sin;
It can be freed if you let Jesus in.

Your heart is cold and hard as a stone;
Jesus can heal it and make it His own.

Don't be afraid, or feel you don't know how to start;
Cry out to Jesus and He'll do His part.

He's patiently waiting for you to give in;
Just crack the door open and let Him begin.

He'll send in His spirit to kindle a spark;
The fire will spread and fill up your heart.

As your heart overflows with the love Jesus gives;
You'll know without doubt that your new heart lives.

Jesus has claimed you and made you His own;
In newness of life, you're no longer alone.

Revelation 3:20   Behold, I stand at the door and knock: if any man hear my voice, and open the door, I will come into him, and will sup with him, and he with me.

A New Song

How can you fight when you can't even see?
You're a slave to sin and think that you're free.

The god of this world has blinded your eyes;
Put a veil over your heart, by telling you lies.

You think that you're clothed in silk and in lace;
Truth is, your body's as bare as your face.

You stand there defenseless; no weapons of war;
You stepped out in the cold and then shut the door.

The thief comes to steal, kill, and destroy;
The control of your life brings him nothing but joy.

He plays on his pipe a hypnotic tune;
And bids you, come, follow me to your doom.

Stop for a moment and open your ears;
Could it be, there's a new song that you hear?

A song that's uplifting, enriching your soul;
Says, "Come follow me and I'll make you whole..."

"Stay on this path, and you'll wind up dead;
But, I'll give you life abundant instead!"

John 10:10 The thief cometh not, but for to steal, and to kill, and to destroy: I am come that they might have life, and that they might have it more abundantly.

Father Knows Best

Sometimes I wonder, even out loud;
Is trouble and doubt what life's all about?

Are we here on this earth our lessons to learn;
No matter how many times we get burned?

The spirit is willing, but the flesh is so weak;
How many times must I go down in defeat?

My soul is sinking down into despair;
I find myself grasping and gasping for air.

I cry out to Jesus; I say, "Lord, how long?
How many times must I try to be strong?
How many times do I just carry on?"

The Lord takes my hand and says, "Sit a spell;
You're weak and you're weary; this I know well."

"You're breaking my heart with your fears and your doubts;
Why must you try to figure it out?"

"You're already equipped for each trial you must face;
All that you need is supplied through My grace."

"Cease from your striving and enter your rest;
Believe in your heart that Father knows best."

Hebrews 4:16 Let us therefore come boldly unto the throne of grace, that we may obtain mercy, and find grace to help in time of need.

Open Your Heart -- Order Form

Use this convenient order form to order additional of:
Open Your Heart

Please Print:

Name _____

Address _____

City _____ State _____

Zip _____

Phone ( ) _____

___ copies of book @ $ 12.95 each $ _____
Postage and handling @ $ 3.25 per book $ _____
Minnesota residents add 6.5% tax $ _____
Total amount enclosed $ _____

Make checks payable to Poetry in Pictures

Send to: Poetry in Pictures
P.O. Box 726
Belgrade, MN 56312

You may also order online at www.poetryinpictures.com